"HELPING FAMILIES HEAL, ONE QUILT AT A TIME

The Work of My Heart

17 families share their stories of loss and healing

JENNI SIPE

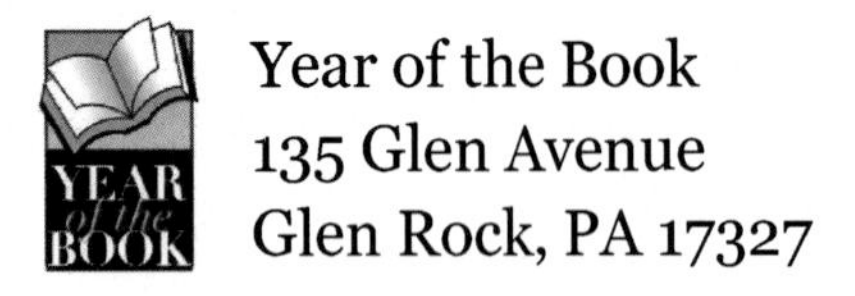

Year of the Book
135 Glen Avenue
Glen Rock, PA 17327

ISBN 10: 1-945670-37-1
ISBN 13: 978-1-945670-37-4

DEDICATION

I am forever grateful to Leslie Delp for nurturing my spirit along this exciting journey. Her encouragement and belief helped me reach out and trust those early and uncertain steps.

Olivia's House
A GRIEF AND LOSS
CENTER FOR CHILDREN
"Hearts can Heal"
"Wings"
"Little Ones"
830 South George

FOREWORD

Jenni has created such a wonderful resource that reminds us that "healing through bereavement" is wrapped up in telling our story." When we share the history of our relationships in art, literature or even quilts, we create a legacy for our loved ones. This book identifies many legacies preserved in the tapestries woven with love! I am proud to have been a part of this insightful resource produced through love and clothing scraps.

~Leslie Delp, M.A., Founder and Bereavement Specialist,
Olivia's House, York, PA

QUILTS: THE WORK OF MY HEART

What a privilege it is to make healing quilts for families who have experienced loss. Many who are represented in this book have endured the painful death of someone they loved deeply. My heart would break each time I heard a new family story. Yet I was also uplifted by their courage to give voice and expression to their experiences.

Over subtle passages of time, each family carefully selected pieces of well-worn clothing, fabrics, and mementos from their loved one's life. They brought these items to me in bags and boxes, and in a quiet light-filled space, we sat together, shared tears and laughter, and reminisced. From this sacred place, the stirring inspiration for my designs evolved. I truly feel honored each time I am invited to create a special story quilt that will become someone's keepsake for generations.

In the pages that follow, you will read stories told by families who have suffered the loss of a loved one, and learn through pictures how they have chosen to celebrate that person's life with custom handmade quilts and pillows.

I know without a doubt this is my mission on earth – to use my love and God-given talent to help families heal.

~ Jenni Sipe, author and quilter

MY HUMBLE BEGINNINGS

Little did I know at six years old sitting in a wagon on a homemade quilt with my two younger sisters, I would discover the beginning of my life's passion. I can still see and smell that quilt – warm from the afternoon sun, musty from the morning dampness, its stuffing escaping from the corners. It was a simple, whole cloth tied quilt, faded red, coarse yet functional that softened our bottoms from the rough floor of the wagon.

The farm where I grew up

My parents and grandparents owned adjoining farms where they grew tomatoes for local canning houses. My responsibility was to look after my sisters while our parents were working in the fields.

Childhood memories really form who we become as grownups, though it's not until later in life that we realize it. It's important to acknowledge our past, whether it's to learn from mistakes or pass on memories to our children and grandchildren.

My two sisters and me – I am the tallest.

Our family.

A Stewartstown, Pennsylvania native, I've been designing and creating quilts and pillows for about 40 years. I inherited my artistic talent from my mom – inspirations for my designs from growing up on the family farms. My love of sewing and fabric began with making doll clothes out of flowered feed sacks on my grandma's treadle sewing machine.

I've always been crafty – such as making Christmas wreaths out of crowsfoot and ground pine found in the woods. My mom sold those wreaths to people she worked with. My Aunt Betty gave me colored crepe paper to make flowers which I then sold to kids in my elementary school for twenty-five cents.

After trying different crafts throughout the years, I discovered quilting in 1975 when residents of our small town helped make squares for a quilt to celebrate America's 200th anniversary. After that first taste, I went on to make patchwork potholders, pillows, and other quilted items and then sold them at craft fairs. Some customers would send photos of their homes or farms and I would recreate those images in appliqué and hand stitching to make wall quilts.

When my son Grant was in elementary school, he played baseball with a boy named KC. While they played, KC's mom Leslie Delp – who is a grief and loss therapist – and I talked about the quilts I made. Leslie said, "I think some of the families who come to me for help would benefit from wrapping up in a quilt while they are grieving. Your work could help them remember their loved one who has passed away."

In 2001, Leslie called to tell me she had quit her job at a hospice center. Coincidentally, I had recently lost my own job at a garden center, and Leslie declared, "Okay Jenni, this was God's plan all along." In April of that year, Leslie and I founded "PIECES OF LOVE" healing quilts and worked together using her wise words and my creative talent to meet with grieving families.

The following year, Leslie opened Olivia's House – A Grief and Loss Center for Children in York, Pennsylvania – a dream of hers since her first child was stillborn. Now Leslie refers families to me when she thinks they would benefit from having a quilt or pillow made from clothing of their loved ones who have passed away.

In 2005, Olivia's House presented "Healing Hearts Through Arts – A Triumphant Experience of the Human Spirit" at the Pullo Family Performing Arts Center at the Penn State York campus. This show featured a fine art exhibit "Imagination and Healing" by more than 50 local artists and an exhibit showing quilts I had made for 11 area families.

I worked on quilts and pillows in a little section of my living room for more years than I care to remember. I really don't know how I was able to design and create in such a small space, but it's all I had to work with. That same small space is where I met with families to talk about quilts and pillows they wanted made in memory of their loved ones. Now it's my "reading room."

Through the generosity of my late parents, in 2004 I built a studio on the back of my home. I am so very grateful! It's big – 20' x 20', bright and cheery with three big windows. I can look out at my backyard where I grow lots of flowers and feed the birds and a rabbit or two. Sometimes even a deer may show up.

My studio.

On the outside of my studio door, I wrote in gold permanent marker, the words of Jeremiah 29:11 that says: “For I know the plans I have for you,” declares the Lord, “plans to prosper you and not to harm you, plans to give you hope and a future.”

What a blessing it is!

MY GRANDMA'S STORY

BERTHA INEZ BLEVINS DUTTON

I spent a lot of time with my grandma as a child growing up on the family farms. While my two sisters helped our parents in the fields baling hay and straw and planting vegetables, I begged to stay inside with my grandma and Aunt Robena to help around the house. I remember the luscious angel food cake she made from scratch using a dozen fresh eggs I had just gathered from the chickens, and the yellow layer cake with creamy coconut icing served with her own canned peaches she made for Sunday company – usually her sister Maude and husband Charlie.

Grandma

Grandma in her garden.

I called my grandma "Maw Maw." Her husband, my "Paw Paw," was a mean old Mister. My two sisters and I were scared of him. When he wasn't working around the farm, he could be found watching baseball on a little black and white television in the family room of the old farm house.

Legend says my grandparents bought the farm for a little bit of nothing because a man had once hung himself in the barn.

My grandma had special sayings for everything. If I fussed about boyfriends or the lack of them, she would say, "Well dear, there's other fish in the sea." When I had children and was overwhelmed by their bad behavior, she would say,

"You'll just have to throw them over one shoulder and catch them on the other one."

Grandma's basketball team.

Grandma was born in 1900 in southwest Virginia, one of seven children. Her mama would knit wool socks for six of the children, but had to knit cotton ones for my grandmother because she was allergic to wool. Grandma played on a girl's basketball team when she was in high school, but her desire was to become a nurse. Her parents told her that being a nurse was not a proper vocation for a woman so sadly she did not follow her dream. She saw so many changes in her lifetime and passed away in 1995 at the age of 94.

I made this special quilt in 2001 to honor her life. The quilt is hand appliquéd and hand quilted. The honeysuckle surrounding her fabric "portrait" grew on the banks of the farm roads, and the red geraniums in the four corners were her favorite flower.

Grandma's quilt I made in 2002.

In 2016, I made this 32” square in honor of the time I spent with my grandma in the kitchen. The quilt is hand appliquéd and hand quilted and includes all of the animals I grew up with on the farm.

“Grandma and me” quilt.

KRISTOPHER'S STORY

by Leslie Delp, M.A.

Leslie and Ken's wedding photo.

When I learned I would never get to dress my baby in the clothes I had purposefully collected, I was devastated. The Slippery Rock State College outfit was picked out especially to surprise my husband, as he was an alumnus. The little sneakers that fit on my thumb, the t-shirt that said "Daddy's Handsome Boy" – so many clothes bought with excitement and anticipation.

When a doctor tells you that your baby has died, all your hopes and dreams die instantly as well. That is not to say you don't visit those dreams again and again... especially as the calendar rolls around the following year to the anniversary, the very day you were told.

Parents who lose a child naturally follow their child's age. It is what we do. It is not right or wrong, it just is. Every year you imagine what they would look like one year older, what they would be doing if they had lived, what special attributes they would have because they were your child.

Having my quilt made from Kristopher's clothes, and some of my own clothes from that time in my life, is so therapeutic. Kristopher was our first baby. His brother and sister did not know him and this quilt is a tangible way for them to learn about and remember him.

My husband and I struggled after his death and worked hard to find meaning in the experience we had been through. He and I consider Kristopher to be the glue that holds our marriage together. We feel blessed that he came into our lives for the short time he did.

Leslie and Ken with KC and Lyndsay.

Now because of his life, I opened a children's grief and loss center in our community that helps others as they walk the lonely journey of bereavement. My husband assisted me in creating this center for children and their families when they lose a loved one. We provide all services at no cost and it is a meaningful tribute to Kristopher, like this memory quilt.

Detail of Leslie's quilt.

Leslie's quilt.

BRADY'S STORY

by Kim Patterson Tome

Kim, Brady, Jacob, and Luke.

Brady Woodrow Patterson was born November 1, 1965, in York, Pennsylvania. He was the third of five children born to Joy and Parker Patterson, Jr. Brady graduated in 1983 from Red Lion High School and was working on his B.A. from Penn State. He met a girl named Kimberly Staub and on September 24, 1988, they were married.

They shared sixteen remarkable years together and were blessed with so much. What a joy it was for Brady to become a daddy when God sent them two unbelievable children – Luke W. and Jake W. Patterson. He was their hero. To them, their daddy could climb mountains.

Brady had an unforgettable smile, and his joking was inescapable. He was a warm and giving friend to many and was always ready to help in a time of need. So full of life and energy, Brady lived life to the fullest. He treasured the simple things, such as time spent playing with his boys, fishing, and being with family. He thanked God everyday for his beautiful boys, his wonderful wife, family and friends.

On Tuesday evening, June 17, 2003, Brady displayed his final loving act for his family as he shielded his son from injury while their car slid on slippery, rain-covered roads. We don't always understand why God deems it necessary to take a loved one so early in life. But for the family, Brady will always be their hero. They are sure he would want to tell them with his ever present smile, "I'm fine and I'll always be with you."

> "When I lost the love of my life so tragically at a young age, I was broken. Nothing could ever take away the crippling pain, but you eventually find things to help soothe it. I did everything in my power to keep Brady alive in the souls of our boys. I'll always remember helping Jacob and Luke pick out pieces of clothing that defined who their daddy was to them. The quilts are a forever reminder of his love and passion for life I will always have a sense of warmth and peace knowing our sons have this special memoir forever."
> *~Kimberly Patterson Tome*

> "I was just 4 years old when my dad died. Over the years, the quilt has given me many ways to find happiness and security. Having all those pieces of clothing my dad wore gives me a sense of peace. I can reconnect by the smell or just laying with it when I feel alone. It's amazing what pieces of fabric can do for someone." *~Jacob Patterson*

> "At 7 years old, I lost the best person in my life – my dad. When my mom had the quilt made for me, I wasn't really sure how I wanted to use it. At first I just laid it at the foot of my bed so each night I could imagine jumping into bed with my dad. The quilt stayed there for a couple of years until I grew more and started kicking it onto the floor at night. I didn't want that so I folded it neatly so only my dad's picture was showing. Later I stood the quilt against the wall on my TV stand. To this day, it still sits in the same place facing my door so that every day I wake up or walk into my room, my dad is staring right at me with his "shitty" grin." *~Luke Patterson*

YORK
HARLEY-DAVIDSON
YORK, PENNSYLVANIA
THE LEGENDARY
Boot Hill
Saloon
Biketoberfest
across from the cemetery
DAYTONA BEACH, FL
Bike Week
DAYTONA USA
WORLD'S LARGEST
MOTORCYCLE EVENT
1996
ALAMO CITY
HARLEY-DAVIDSON
San Antonio
TEXAS
DEMO
Harley-Davidson
TOUR 2002
PITTSBURGH
Press, Tank & Fender Depts.
It Ain't For Everyone
NITTANY LIONS
PENN STATE
THE PENNSYLVANIA STATE UNIVERSITY
Penn State

Luke's quilt.

Jacob's quilt.

TODD'S STORY

by Tracey Leik

Todd Christopher Leik was born on December 19, 1969. His birthday was six days before Christmas and he always accused his parents of taking his gifts from under the tree and rewrapping them for his birthday because they ran out of time. To this day, the boys and I always wait to pick out our Christmas tree on his birthday.

When Todd was four years old, he developed severe asthma which continued throughout his life, but it never stopped him. He pushed himself to participate in any sport or activity that interested him. Being athletic, Todd ran hurdles for Eastern York's track team and also played football there. He wore the same number as his older brother Jack – Number 43. There was a joke among the team members that the yardage Corey Nicholas gained during a game, Todd would lose in penalties!

Todd, Tracey, Wyatt, and Dalton.

He graduated from Eastern York High School in 1987 and took courses at Penn State's York campus. The Dallas Cowboys became his favorite football team –he considered himself a cowboy at heart, right down to his hat and boots.

We met in our early twenties and married October 3, 1992. Our son Wyatt was born in 1996 and Dalton arrived in 1999, completing our beautiful family. Our household also included our two dogs, Buca a schnauzer, and Buzz a German shorthair pointer. Todd loved to fish and hunt. He would walk down to Kreutz Creek with his tackle box and rod. He spent many hours in the woods hunting. He loved nature and passed this love on to both of our boys. When Todd was young he always said, "When I grow up, I want to get married and have kids so I can always get new toys."

Now he had his boys and new toys.

Right after we were married, Todd got a job with the York County Assessment Office. He made lots of friends along the way and moved up the ladder quickly. He was promoted to the director of the assessment office and was also the chief assessor.

Todd loved to swim and always wore bright yellow trunks. His father in law (my stepdad) owned a charter business and Todd learned how to scuba dive so we could dive together. We had many good times being with family.

Todd's dream was to build a log cabin for us. We had the plans drawn up and purchased a scenic lot high on a hill in the Mt. Pisgah area when he got sick. On August 28, 2002, Todd passed away after a courageous battle with cancer. He was well liked and many friends and co-workers attended his funeral. The church was so full that people had to stand in the back during the service.

Several people suggested making quilts for Wyatt and Dalton from Todd's clothing after he passed away. Since my sewing skills were limited to replacing buttons and simple mending I knew the quilts were not something I was able to attempt myself. Then Leslie Delp, founder of Olivia's House – A Grief and Loss Center for Children – introduced me to Jenni Sipe. We met and discussed ideas for the quilts. I knew they were going to become treasured works of art but never imagined how beautiful they would be. I gathered all of Todd's clothes including a multitude of neckties, and Jenni fashioned them into four colorful memory quilts representing his life.

Jenni made two 50"x 60" quilts for Wyatt and Dalton who were six and two and a half years old when their dad died. On Wyatt's quilt, the scene is a log cabin and a pond with him and his dad fishing. Dalton's quilt also has a log cabin with him and his dad hunting. Jenni also made quilts for Todd's parents and his nephew Jake. Each quilt is similar, but at the same time very unique and personalized. All of the beautiful quilts are loving memories of Todd and dearly beloved treasures like no other. Jenni is an extremely talented artist who truly creates works from the heart.

Wyatt's quilt.

Dalton's quilt.

STAN'S STORY

by Susan Houser

Stan and I met at York College in York, Pennsylvania. I was a freshman and he was a sophomore. His ambition was to become a French teacher. We got married in 1969 after dating about a year. Stan substitute taught during a teacher strike and decided to change his major to business. He was very successful in this profession and in the 1980s at the height of his career, he had a five-state territory selling electronic components.

Susan and Stan Hauser.

He had many challenging illnesses during our marriage. He contracted meningitis in 1988 and thankfully recovered. In 2004, he was diagnosed with pneumonia and was on a respirator for almost a week. We almost lost him that time.

In 2008, I saw his health declining due to a low-grade infection. He was not interested in going to a physician. I finally convinced him to see a doctor on Monday, November 10 and he was diagnosed with a "cold."

The next morning, he mentioned his throat felt funny and said he was going to lie down. I followed him into the bedroom where he fell into bed and his limbs were going cold. I immediately called 9-1-1 and attempted to give CPR. When the EMTs arrived, they worked on him in the ambulance. We got to the hospital and within a half hour, the terrible news came that he had not survived. It was congestive heart failure. You can imagine my shock and grief!

I was later delivering *Mary Kay* products and visiting with a customer when she asked about the death of my husband. She had known him because he had been active in my business delivering and mailing products and running errands. She offered Jenni's information and encouraged me to call her about a memory quilt.

The quilt is beautiful! Our daughter Brenda found comfort in having it with her, especially during long nights that first year after Stan passed away. We are both reminded of the years of memories created together as a family. A few of the squares in the quilt are from places we traveled with *Mary Kay* – Bermuda and Germany to name a few. Many of the squares represent Stan's hobbies of playing drums, music, boating, and his Corvette. Others are from favorite places like York College, places he enjoyed eating, and clothing gifts from his family. Jenni also created a pillow for me and it is cherished.

Susan, Stan and daughter Brenda.

Brenda said, "I can't thank Jenni enough for this quilt. It has brought me so much comfort since my dad's passing. I keep it hanging on its own rack in my dining room. When I'm having a really bad day or missing him greatly, I often sleep with it. I look at certain patches and recall special memories. I thank my mom for having the idea to have it made and I thank Jenni for putting so much care and thought into it."

Susan's pillow (front and back).

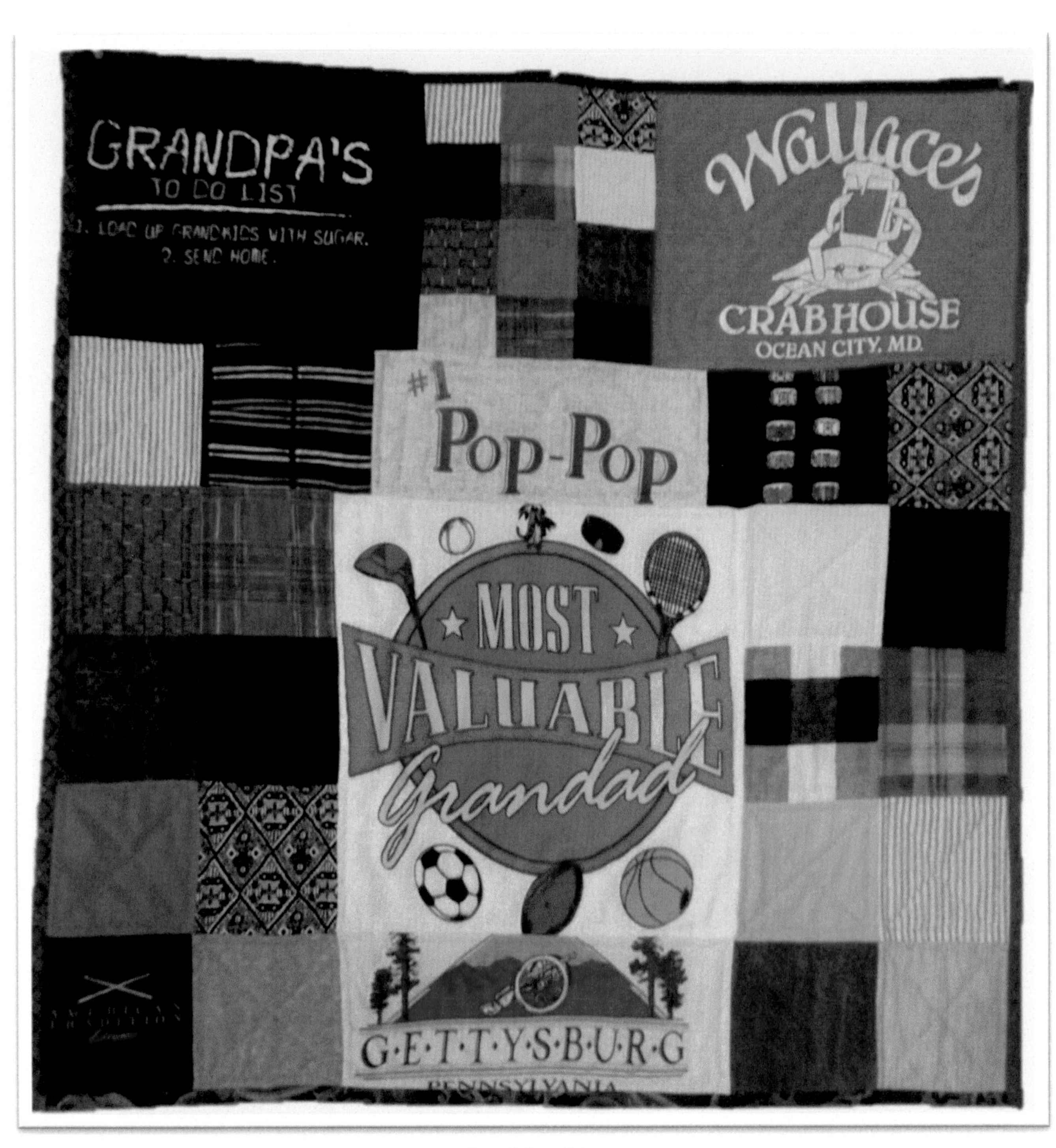

Brenda's quilt.

SCOTT'S STORY

by Donna Luczak Robertson

Scott Allen Robertson was born on January 11, 1984, our first child. He was a chubby baby, one that drew comments from passersby about what a "healthy big boy" he was. Precocious and inquisitive from the start, by the time he was two, he was talking in full sentences and stringing them together almost non-stop. He loved books from an early age and by ten months would give one his full attention for 20-30 minutes.

Scott and sister Kelly.

He always had a vivid imagination and loved to "dress up" in his play. He would don my boots and his dad's gloves and pretend to be a fire fighter, or put a basket on his head to be a football player! He outgrew that chubby baby body and was 6'3" and lean by the time he was 17. He became a very likeable young man – gentle, with an easy smile, kind and funny. Scott was a really good student, excelled in writing, and was active in the drama department in high school. He played the trumpet in middle school and the acoustic and electric bass guitar in high school.

Scott always had a close relationship with his only sibling Kelly who was 22 months younger. She always looked up to him and they were very good friends. As older children they never argued and played well with each other from the time she was able to crawl.

Scott had just begun college at the University of North Carolina-Wilmington on a full honor scholarship in the fall of 2001. He aspired to be a writer and was

Scott, Donna, Roger, and Kelly.

constantly scribbling down story ideas. The university was close to the beach and he seemed to be taking root in his new college surroundings.

Our family was together in mid-October for Scott's fall break. He had what appeared to be an intestinal bug, but it wasn't enough to keep him from enjoying our trip to Myrtle Beach or game nights with the extended family.

When he returned to school, his asthma was bothering him. On Friday, October 26, 2001, he got a ride home for the weekend and had a "weird rash" on his arms and feet. Other than being tired and having the rash, he seemed fine and since the doctor's office was already closed we waited until Saturday to go to urgent care. The doctors there thought it might be Rocky Mountain spotted fever, so they started him on an antibiotic. By Sunday, Scott had flu like symptoms – nausea, vomiting, fatigue and backache. By Monday and Tuesday he had not improved and was still vomiting. The doctor's office said to give it time. By Tuesday evening he got worse and we took him to the hospital where he was given IV fluids and discharged.

At 7 AM Wednesday, October 31, I found Scott unresponsive in his bed with his pupils fixed and dilated. We called 9-1-1 and he was taken to the emergency room where we were told he had a rare form of cancer – acute T-cell leukemia, and was brain dead. This form of leukemia apparently moves quickly and because he was a healthy young man, everyone missed it. He died within several hours of his arrival at the hospital and we were devastated, stunned, angry, and in disbelief. The rash? Petechial hemorrhages from the leukemia.

My cousin Lynn Hunter had always been a part of my life. She was one of my "in town cousins" growing up and almost every childhood holiday memory includes something of "Lynnie." She is eight years my senior so I always looked up to my "cool big cousin." She had seen an article in her local paper about Jenni's quilts and asked if I would like to have one made in Scott's memory. This was a very appealing idea because I knew I could not throw away Scott's clothing. I asked Scott's sister Kelly if she would like one as well and she did. We chose some "fill in" fabrics that spoke to us. We gathered Scott's clothing and Kelly, Lynn and I went to visit Jenni to work out the designs of the two quilts.

Kelly's quilt accompanied her through the remainder of high school, through college and graduate school and is well loved and handled. Mine has been in a beautiful box that my father-in-law made just for this purpose. I found that although I love looking at the quilt on occasion –it's beautiful and I am glad that I have it – I just can't have it out all the time. It is too hard! I don't want anything to happen to it - to fade or tear – so I can be assured of having it forever. So in the box it stays. I see this box in our family room every day, but I don't open it unless I'm ready. I am grateful to Lynn for giving me the opportunity to have it and to Jenni's skilled hands in crafting its beauty.

Most of the squares are from Scott's favorite t-shirts. Some are from "fancier" shirts he bought in his senior year for after-graduation parties. Others are from favorite things like his gray terry-cloth robe. There is one fabric, an orange and brown print on a white background that was from Kelly's favorite blouse at the time of Scott's death. They were so close that we wanted to include some of "her" in his quilt.

One square includes copies of embroidery that are from Scott's Army-issue knapsack that he carried with him everywhere. In his junior year, he wanted me

The quilt box.

Robertson family quilt.

to teach him how to embroider some pictures on it so I did. Some of the pictures are ones he drew and some were drawn by his friends. I put them on green fabric to mimic his bag and Jenni incorporated them into the quilt.

The central "Tree of Life" motif is a favorite of mine and I wanted to have a way for the quilt to tell a story about what Scott was like. I asked friends and family members to give me one word that made them think of Scott and had them embroidered on some of the tree leaves.

Embroidered handprint and poem.

The poem is one I found in a catalog that spoke to me about the circumstances of Scott's leaving too quickly and unexpectedly. The handprint is an embroidered version of one Scott left on a wall of an abandoned building. His girlfriend Robin was able to make a tracing of it for me.

In 2015, 14 years after his death, I was finally able to sort through the rest of collected things from his life and gave many of them to new homes to be played with and brought back to life. It's a process and I like to think my quilt was one of the stepping stones that got me here.

CAITLIN'S STORY

by parents Marty and Alex Dunbar

Caitlin Dunbar was born March 9, 1989, and passed away on December 28, 2004.

For 15 and 3/4 years, Caitlin lived a very full and rich life. She was always friendly, smiling and happy. Caitlin was kind, considerate and able to sense the needs of others. She could talk confidently with anyone of any age, and was independent with a strong sense of self.

Caitlin had a very special relationship with her dad who was her full time at-home parent from age 2 years on. Both of them were night-owls and would stay up late watching a movie, reading books, or just talking. Throughout her life, she always had at least one of her parents, usually her dad, tuck her into bed.

At age 6, Caitlin became a big sister when Kelsey was adopted from China. Three years later, she accompanied her dad to Vietnam for the adoption of her youngest sister Kristy. She was actively involved in both of her sisters' lives.

Dunbar family.

Caitlin was a Girl Scout who loved all things outdoors. Her favorite destination was Girl Scout Summer Camp. One of her goals in life was to become a camp counselor. Disney World was a frequent destination. She loved to travel and also visited throughout the United States, Bermuda, Canada, Mexico, Vietnam, and Thailand.

High school brought Caitlin back to her passion from her younger years – dance. Her final dance recital was on December 17, 2004. Her journal entry read: "So yesterday was my dance performance at school. It was soo much fun! i can't wait till the next one which is in the spring. i did really well and wish i could do it again..."

A week later, on December 24, 2004, she had her wisdom teeth removed. They had become impacted and were bothering her. She decided she had time during winter break to recover rather than losing time during the school year. The procedure went well and she came home ready to rest. Two days later, she was not feeling well and appeared dehydrated. When Caitlin stumbled and fell, we called 9-1-1 and took her to the emergency room. The early diagnosis was that Caitlin had a sepsis infection (pretty bad stuff) and would need blood work.

They decided to airlift her to Johns Hopkins Hospital in Baltimore. Hopkins said Caitlin could have any number of things going on. After additional blood work, acute promyelocytic leukemia (APL) was diagnosed. The oncologists met with us and said this form of leukemia was highly survivable. However, if a patient died, it was usually in the first week because they could not stabilize them. APL is rare in children. There are about 50 new cases in the United States each year – most children are between 2 and 3 years of age. For the next 24 hours, doctors, nurses and specialists worked feverishly to keep Caitlin alive. And then she was gone.

Over the years since her death, Caitlin's family and friends have kept her memory alive through numerous projects. Caitlin loved to write poetry. Both her high school and her former elementary school held poetry contests in her memory. A dance award program was created in her honor at her high school. A scholarship recognizing girls who had completed their Girl Scout Gold Award project was sponsored at her high school. Caitlin's spirit is most alive in the Girl Scouts of Central Maryland's Caitlin Dunbar Nature Center. It was created by several of her friends and has expanded to two locations. They are maintained by many people who have found themselves drawn to the project. Kids who did not know Caitlin and many who were not even born when she was alive have been active in expanding the nature center.

Lynn Hunter, Caitlin's former music teacher at Fulton Elementary School referred us to Jenni about a year after Caitlin died. Lynn's nephew had died of acute leukemia and his family had a quilt made by Jenni. Gazing upon the quilt stirs up fond memories of some of Caitlin's favorite things in life. Each of the clothing items selected for the quilt have special stories associated with them including Girl Scout vests, a Swiss Army shirt, Disney characters, Rehoboth Beach dresses, roller coasters and roses, her favorite flower.

Dunbar family at Disney.

Dunbar family quilt.

BLANCHE'S STORY

by daughter Sharon Hartenstein

Sharon Hartenstein with mother Blanche.

My mother, Blanche Arabelle (Richey) Bamforth was a native of the Glen Rock, Pennsylvania area and was raised in Centerville. She was the sixth child in a family of nine girls and one boy.

She loved Glen Rock and was proud to tell everyone she was a homebody. She loved walking and as a young girl walked many miles in the surrounding area to Sunday School picnics. My mother and father raised their family in Glen Rock and she walked many miles between Centerville and Glen Rock visiting and taking care of my grandparents. She loved to cook and baked birthday cakes for her family and grandchildren. There was always a cake from "Mamaw" on a special occasion. She was a good listener and a wonderful mother

Jenni was introduced to me by my daughter Jennifer Hartenstein McGraw. Jenni made a crazy quilt for Jennifer with her uncle Richard Hartenstein's clothing and personal accents.

The quilt from my mother's clothing is truly unique and is enjoyed by the entire family. Jenni placed cardinals and snow in the center as a focal point. My mother loved cardinals, winter and shoveling snow. The sneakers signify her love of walking. She was a coupon clipper and saver and would tell others that clipping coupons was her "hobby" My mother and I prepared many Thanksgiving dinners so Jenni placed a turkey and a cake on the quilt. Another hobby of my mother's was collecting pitchers so one was placed on the quilt with a bingo card. She loved bingo and played until she died. There is a coffee cup on the quilt because she loved coffee. My mother and I shared many cups of coffee and cappuccino over her lifetime.

Jenni's handiwork is a tribute to mom's life and I am so glad to have it It is a wonderful quilt of happiness and memories and when I look at the squares, I remember her wearing the shorts, shirts, slacks, pjs, sweaters, and robes. Her hankies and pillowcases are in the quilt as well. I know my daughter Jennifer and her daughter Stella will treasure it.

I also had a pillow made for Blanche's eldest great granddaughter Grace Elizabeth Hartenstein. Grace is the daughter of my late son Jim Hartenstein III and his wife Tami Sechrist Hartenstein.

Grace's pillow.

Sharon's quilt.

FRANK HOMMOWUN'S STORY

by Ann Hoffman, "#2 daughter," (as Dad would say)

Young Frank Hommowun.

My father, Frank Robert Hommowun, was born on September 10, 1917, in Oak Park, Cook County, Illinois, and died on March 27, 2002, in Palo Alto, California. He lived a rich and productive life, always mindful of his responsibilities to his wife and family.

My mother and father both grew up during the Great Depression and learned the life skills to survive. I believe many their age learned to save, scrimp, and make do with what they had and put raising their children at the top of the list. For years my parents did without to provide for me and my sisters and to always have some reserves for emergencies.

Dad graduated from Virginia Polytechnic Institute in 1939 as a mechanical engineer. Today the school is known as Virginia Tech. He met my mother there while she was taking classes in secretarial skills. Two years after his graduation, my parents married on July 1, 1941. My maternal grandfather thought my dad might not "amount to much" because he was a little too fun loving and a jokester. But that changed after his time overseas in the military. War gives one a different perspective on life.

My older sister was 4 when my parents married. Since daddy went directly into the U.S. Army Air Corps after graduation, my parents chose to wait to start their family, thinking he would soon go overseas. After a year, they decided he was staying state-side so I came along in 1943. Surprise, surprise, he was sent to France shortly after my birth.

Upon returning from France and leaving the Air Corps (later called the Air Force) behind as a possible full-time career choice, my family moved to New Jersey, and in 1948 my sister Patty was born.

Dad worked for Worthington Corporation there until 1958. During his travels for Worthington, Dad decided if the opportunity came along, he would love to live permanently in California. A job came up as a sales representative in San Francisco and the family moved to Palo Alto, California. That job only lasted two years. When the company wanted to move us back east again, he said, "No thanks," and we stayed in Palo Alto. Dad then got a job working for Lockheed. After nearly ten years he was let go during a large layoff. Boeing and Lockheed were known for letting go of thousands at a time. He and another man went to court and sued, knowing they had been riffed because of their age and before they would have worked long enough to receive a pension. The two men won their suit and Dad got a small pension after he turned 65.

After Lockheed, he returned to school for additional education and re-invented himself. He started working for the San Jose School District as a Vo Tech counselor. He was very successful, helping students with jobs and education and seemed to be well respected by the students.

After retirement he played some golf with friends for a while but then settled into reading, as well as his new found fascination with the computer, genealogy, and studying countries and places he wanted to visit. During the early years when my parents couldn't afford to travel, daddy spent hours reading train timetables and flight schedules. He was always working on another place to go and see. He really would have made an excellent travel agent. He was a social person and enjoyed sharing his findings.

During the time we lived on the east coast, daddy never took a vacation because his time off from work was spent in the Air Force Reserves. Those Reserve obligations helped provide extra money for orthodontics for my older sister and savings for college. He retired as a Lt. Colonel which added to his retirement income.

After his daughters were grown and living away from home, my parents started to travel. All those years of study really paid off. My parents traveled a great deal in the United States by car and plane, as well as out of the country by cruising or planned land trips after flying to their destination.

During their travels, they also included the family. Around 1992, mother and daddy took my younger sister Patty and me to London, York, and Liverpool in the UK, then on to the European continent traveling by bus. This was our first overseas adventure although my older sister Betty had previously traveled abroad with my parents and her husband.

In 1995, dad's daughters and sons-in-law were included on a cruise through the Panama Canal with various land stops on the way. In July of 2001, the eight of us cruised from San Francisco through the inner passage of Alaska and back for our parent's 60th wedding anniversary. It was a great celebration, but also sad because we realized it would probably be dad's last grand trip, which it was.

I met Jenni around 2002. I learned of her work with grieving families and documenting wonderful memories for them through the quilts she made. After my dad died, I contacted Jenni and started the process for a very special quilt for my mom and sisters.

The quilt Jenni made for them illustrates some of the many destinations where my parents traveled. It also depicts the "vanity license plate" my sisters and I got him for a birthday gift. His computer (which really looks ancient) gave him many hours of enjoyment through looking up trips and studying places to visit and it allowed him to access genealogical information. The quilt also shows the church my parents attended in Palo Alto and his love of watching sports on television.

My mother was touched by the quilt. She enjoyed looking at the "symbols" of the memories and she proudly showed it to family and visitors alike. We hung it over her bed so she always felt Dad's presence. Since her death in 2011, I have had the quilt and as my mother did, enjoy looking at it and remembering.

Hommowun family quilt.

DAVID'S STORY

by Debbie Grobosky

David was born on April 5, 1954. He was the oldest boy of four children. His family relocated often during his childhood due to his father's job with DuPont. He graduated from the University of Connecticut with an Economics degree.

He began his work life as an insurance salesman but soon changed to selling for a corrugated packaging corporation. He found his niche in the business world and won several top sales awards. In later years, he became a sales manager and was able to talk to anyone anywhere about anything. It was a quality that made him shine brightly. I used to tell him moving around as a child must have made him a great conversationalist.

David, Debbie, and son Ryan.

We met while I was working for a local bank. David came in to apply for a mortgage and was seated in my office. His personality, smile and ease of conversation drew me in immediately. During that time we realized we were living in the same apartment complex and the rest was history. We were married in 1982 and blessed with our wonderful son Ryan in 1993.

David was a very involved father, coaching Ryan's soccer team, actively participating in Boy Scouts, and lending a hand at school when needed. School fundraising challenges were always fun. Ryan and "Salesman Dad" would travel the hills of our neighborhood while he shared his expertise on the "art of selling." This time spent together helped Ryan achieve "top salesman" of his elementary class. It is one of the memories Ryan treasures.

David loved sports and cheered for his favorite football team, the Buffalo Bills, no matter how many times they lost. He loved cars and cherished his 1985 Monte Carlo SS. He took Ryan for rides on Sunday afternoons so they could have "guy time". He looked forward to working in the yard because it was a job that could be finished and admired. Vacation time at the beach was his favorite relaxation. A fun day was riding the waves with Ryan while wearing his wild outdated swim trunks that made us laugh.

One day in 2003 everything changed when David was diagnosed with lung cancer at age 49. He was not a smoker so it caught us by surprise. He began the fight of his life with radiation and chemotherapy. He never complained and took the bad days in stride, but he continued to decline. His battle and suffering ended after three months when he passed away peacefully, surrounded by his family.

It is difficult to describe David in a few paragraphs but simply stated he was a wonderful husband, father, son, brother, co-worker, and friend who was admired by others and taken away too soon. He was a kind, loving, funny and courageous man who brought a quiet strength to our family. David is greatly missed and remains in our hearts forever.

A close friend first brought the idea of a memory quilt to my attention. She told me about the wonderful healing program at Olivia's House and a special lady named Jenni Sipe who made memory quilts. But it was a huge task and too painful to think about after losing David to cancer just three months earlier.

Debbie and son Ryan today.

Thirteen months later my son Ryan and I had the opportunity to go through the grief and healing program at Olivia's House. After the program, I knew a memory quilt would be something to help us through the grieving process. So Ryan and I began to gather personal items that would tell a story about David. We delivered the clothing and other memorabilia to Jenni and she created a beautiful quilt for us to help our healing journey.

Our quilt is proudly displayed in our home where others can share its artistic beauty and feel the love from which it was created. It is a wonderful memorial and sentimental keepsake that has brought warmth and calmness to our home. It represents strength and hope that continues to help mend our broken hearts. It is a pleasant visual memory of the time we had with David and a reminder that he is always with us.

Ryan's quilt.

BILL'S STORY

by Laura Cowburn

William H Cowburn, Jr., was born in Bainbridge, Maryland, and soon afterwards his parents moved to York, Pennsylvania. His father left and his grandparents raised him and his brother Bob so their mother could work and take care of her own health. He considered himself to be a lifelong resident of York, living in the city and moving to the suburbs later in life.

He was a graduate of William Penn High School in 1972, worked a short time for York Borg-Warner Company and then as a York City Police Cadet. He graduated from York College in 1992 and worked in the Comptroller's office with the Pennsylvania Department of Education and then for the Pennsylvania Employees Retirement System.

Bill and Laura.

Bill and I had a parallel life when we met and fell in love. We both graduated high school in 1972, college in 1992, and had both been married before we met. We took a considerable amount of time getting to know each other, building trust and confidence in our relationship.

When we moved in together in 1998, our relationship was strong and built from our past experiences. We wanted everyone to say, "They lived happily ever after."

I had my dog Rusty before we moved in together and Bill "wasn't so sure about him" I took Rusty with me one time and within minutes, I don't think either one remembered I was there. They became inseparable.

We married on March 2, 2001, in a hot air balloon over Red Rock Canyon, Nevada. We both loved to travel. Together we visited China and London.

Bill and Laura at the Great Wall of China.

We planned to visit every capital city in the United States and document the trips. We drove on these trips because Bill enjoyed the scenery change from state to state. The only one we flew to was Hawaii and we visited there the second time on our 10th anniversary on 2011 to go whale watching and renew our wedding vows. We were able to visit about 20 states.

Bill loved American history and coin collecting. He was an avid numismatist and became well known throughout the country since he spoke regularly at conferences and seminars about various coins and their history. He wrote articles for the *Numismatist*, the *Gobrecht Journal*, the *Centinel* and the *Journal of the Barber Coin Collector's Society*. He won the Wagner Award for dedication to the hobby and several awards for his articles including a Heath Literary Award from ANA for his article "How Rare is Rare". He was most noted for his research and knowledge of trade dollars. He was a member of the American Numismatic Association as well as various local and state associations.

Bill enjoyed playing tennis and watching it on television. He loved to read non-fiction books and biographies of our presidents and noteworthy historical events. He enjoyed growing and canning fresh vegetables from the garden. His favorite drink was Coca-Cola and he drank it regularly. Bill loved the music of Bob Dylan and Frank Sinatra. He knew the words to every Dylan song and I loved listening to him sing along.

In September of 2011, Bill and I had dinner and then I ran an errand. When I got home, he was doubled over in pain saying the same thing had happened after lunch that day but the pain had gone away then. I wanted him to seek medical attention right away, but he wouldn't hear of it. I made him promise to go to the doctor the next day.

He was admitted to the hospital for an appendectomy, but his appendix was fine. They found a tumor at the base of his colon. The tumor was removed, biopsied, and he was diagnosed with Stage 3 colon cancer. This was shocking to us both because he had regular colonoscopies and had been under routine medical care and nothing had been found for three years.

This was one that got away from the medical examinations.

Bill and Laura at Kitty Hawk.

He had regular radiation for more than eight months and in June 2012 the doctor announced the cancer had been reduced by 50% and things were doing well. He continued treatments with another drug and began losing his thick and wavy hair.

In October 2012, we decided to take a trip to Kitty Hawk. He bought two straw hats to wear. That was the last trip we took. In November of that year, he developed a blood clot and was hospitalized. The chemo had to be stopped until he could stabilize. That was when the cancer really spread. Bill's brother Bob and I took shifts taking care of him so I could continue to work. Bill was working too, sometimes at the office and sometimes at home.

He had to stop working in January and in February I stopped working to take care of him 24/7.

Bill with his great niece.

The last picture ever taken of him was with his great niece. On Sunday, February 24, 2013, Bill took his last breath at home with me, his brother Bob and Bob's wife Sue.

His memorial service/funeral was held Saturday, March 2, 2013 – our 12th wedding anniversary. It was a celebration of his life and happiness that his pain was finally over.

I found Jenni through a friend who suggested her to me because I was hoping to do something with Bill's clothing. After meeting with Jenni I realized I wanted a queen size quilt that would cover me at night and give me comfort.

In the middle of the quilt is the t-shirt Bill bought on our last trip. Surrounding it is various articles of clothing from trips and activities – the blood donor shirt, the coin clubs, the emblems of York, PA, the Hawaiian shirts, a Coca-Cola visor from his tennis gear and even a piece of his tennis towel. There are pieces of shirts he wore regularly. One of the shirts – a white, blue, and black striped oxford that was his favorite for weekends - is found in a few places throughout the quilt. The ties used for the edging were also some of his favorites.

I had Jenni embroider "they lived happily ever after" at the bottom of the quilt.

The best part of this experience was that it prompted me to clean out Bill's clothes. Some were easily discarded or donated. Those articles that had meaning went into a box to take to Jenni and I was excited that some of those pieces would become part of a new keepsake for the future. The quilt is perfect and now I have memories of our life together and an heirloom to give to his great niece or great nephew someday.

Laura's quilt.

JOSH'S STORY

by John, Connie, and Lauren Wolfe

Josh and Lauren.

Josh's accident happened on his little sister Lauren's second day of high school. He was in the Kinsley Construction apprenticeship where he was in the classroom for two weeks, then in the field for two weeks. He was on his way to a job site in Reading, PA. The autopsy showed no medical reasons and it was determined he fell asleep and crossed the median.

I actually learned about the accident on TV. While they didn't show his truck, it was one of those motherly instincts. Josh died at the scene. I was home alone when the police came. I called my husband John and our first thought was to get to Lauren and tell her. From there, it was a blur and our family and friends and faith were our strength for months and years to come.

At age 14, Lauren lost her big brother who had proudly watched over her from the day she was born. As we think about Josh, these are the things that describe him: personable, compassionate, jokester, always on the go as a child with no fear, liked to make his sister laugh, liked family camping trips, enjoyed family time when everyone was together especially granny, gramps and his cousin Shane who was 7 hours younger and was like a brother their entire time together.

Josh and his dad.

Josh was a graduate of Central York High School class of 2001 and a volunteer football coach at the time of his death. Since that date of August 28th, 2002, we refer to history as "before Josh's accident" and "after Josh's accident." We established a memorial scholarship at the high school to be awarded to any football players who exemplify Josh's character both on and off the field. It's been a way to keep his memory alive.

John and I cherish the quilt as a reminder of Josh's spirited personality showing his sense of style with bold colors and sports. His football jersey number at Central York High School was 58. That has become our favorite number and we remember it with him in our hearts.

We found Jenni through Leslie Delp at Olivia's House. This is the place we have been connected to since hearing about it. We welcomed her into our home and told her about Josh as we showed her his bedroom all adorned in Pittsburgh Steelers, Pirates, Central York and anything sports related. He LOVED sports! In fact, when he was in elementary school, he would get up early on a Saturday morning and watch ESPN News over and over. As we sorted through Josh's clothes to decide what to include in the quilt, Jenni asked us to tell you about him and it was a comfort to remember when he wore certain things or where he wore them. He loved to make a statement with his clothes and wanted to look his best with his own style.

"The quilt provided comfort when I was away at school and it helped me feel safe whenever I held onto it. The items we picked to make the quilt were pieces of Josh's wardrobe that he wouldn't have wanted us to get rid of – he wore them proudly. I was always proud to show the quilt to my friends. For those that didn't know him, it was a way for them to get a glimpse of his personality. I know this sounds weird but for the longest time it had his scent and that was something I cherished and it helped me feel closer to him." ~Lauren, Josh's sister

Josh, John, Lauren, and Connie.

Lauren's quilt.

JOE'S STORY

by Bev Castriota

Castriota family.

Joe Castriota, Jr., was a wonderful husband and father who was taken away too soon.

His life revolved around his family and friends. He was an inspiration to those around him during his illness. Diagnosed with cancer in October 2001, he fought with courage and dignity for eleven months before losing the battle in September 2002. He left many cherished memories for those who loved him.

I first heard about "healing quilts" from a friend in my support group. I immediately knew I wanted to have quilts made for my three children. Planning the quilts made the task of sorting through Joe's personal things easier. I was able to sit down with Jenni and combine her ideas with mine. Most importantly, the quilts were a way I could fulfill my promise to Joe – to keep his memory alive.

"My quilt completely represents my dad and everything he loved. When I look at my quilt, I can remember him wearing all of the clothing. It is more than pieces of fabric sewn together, it is a collection of memories I can keep forever."

~Angie, Joe's daughter

"The pieces of clothing that make up my quilt are exactly what I remember my dad wearing day after day including his favorite Steelers sweatshirt and those infamous purple 'sauna' shorts. Every part of my quilt has meaning – a meaning I can carry with me forever." *~Stacey, Joe's daughter*

"My quilt is a great way to remember my dad. It holds many memories from all the great times we had golfing and watching Steelers games together. It is a great keepsake I can hold forever." *~ Joey, Joe's son*

Joey's quilt.

UNCLE RICHARD'S STORY

by Jennifer Hartenstein McGraw

My Uncle Dick was born to discover the world and his life was centered around living.

Born Richard Paul Hartenstein, he invited the world to dance, and boy did he lead! Uncle Dick was first and foremost an artist. Because he was a man who had a flare for the original and exquisite, he exposed his family to much in his short meaningful life. Uncle Dick was one of a kind and his tastes reflected that. This quilt is in honor of him. It reflects his life and his personality from the red color on the back to the many pieces of handmade jewelry that adorn the front. The color red which dominates is reminiscent of a big, luxurious bath towel given to him as a Christmas gift. The quilt was purposely designed to reflect the patchwork of his life. The crazy hand stitching represents the craziness he inhaled and exhaled daily as he lived his life in Manhattan.

Family vacations were spent on the shores of Ogunquit, Maine, where Uncle Dick could be spotted bouncing about like a sleek gazelle in his signature black speedos. He had an eye for collectibles and brought many antiques to our little town of New Freedom, Pennsylvania. He lived and worked in New York City and was a makeup artist to famous models and movie stars. He had an abundance of friends there, many who died of AIDS. He moved to the west coast after losing 50 of his friends and was soon after diagnosed with AIDS related complex (ARC) himself. This was Uncle Dick's life of triumph and tragedy.

On the quilt is a red AIDS awareness ribbon and a candle that is always lit to honor him during the holiday season. The self-portrait that adorns the center is an icon he created himself. Every letter sent to us was signed with it.

When Uncle Dick moved to San Diego his clothing style reflected the southwestern United States. The black western style shirt on the quilt evokes many memories.

Jen's quilt.

His *haute couture* jean shirt was so special because it reflected his sense of style and extravagance while revealing the relaxed side of his personality. He was lucky to have so many talented friends who gave him gifts of jewelry and art. Andy Warhol and Ted Muehling were two iconic artists who became an inspiration to Uncle Dick. The thunderbird in the center of the quilt is a symbol that reflects the freedom he displayed in his work and his life. He encouraged us to do big things and he wanted us to spread our wings like that thunderbird.

Uncle Richard.

The heart necklace on the quilt holds special memories because it was created for me on Valentine's Day. It came in the mail with a card that read: "Happy Hearts You and Me. Love, Uncle Dick." It is a gift that will always be special to me and when I wrap up in Uncle Dick's quilt, I am reminded that to have him in my life was to experience true happiness.

GINO'S STORY

by Dana Gladfelter Gaetjen

"Gino" Gladfelter.

There is a saying: "There is not enough darkness in the whole universe to put out the light of one small candle."

Gene's love for his family was that light. He left a legacy following his death on July 31, 2001. Part of that legacy is a family heirloom quilt designed with love by Gene and his wife Dana before his death, for their daughter Gracie.

His life is embodied in the quilt. The center square portrait replicates his beautiful, warm smile that lit up his sun-kissed face. He was known to have a certain "glow" about him after a ride on his bike. To both of his children he left a legacy of hard work, determination, and courage. These character traits are evident in the clothes used to create Gracie's quilt. Gene picked out each piece of clothing for his little girl, knowing they would hold meaning and give comfort when his strong arms could no longer hold her. The colors in the quilt are Gracie's favorites, pink and purple.

Gene and his family took a trip to Disneyworld two months after his confirmed diagnosis of ALS (amyotrophic lateral sclerosis). The Mickey Mouse t-shirt is a reminder of the wonderful time he had introducing Gracie to Mickey and Minnie. In the eyes of his children, Gene was "The World's Best Dad" and he proudly wore this t-shirt for Gracie. As an athlete, Gene was privileged to run and bike in many races in his short life. He was adamant that his children share his passion of using sports as an outlet for negative emotions. He knew that Gracie and her brother Gabe would become wonderful athletes.

Gracie and Leslie Delp holding quilt.

Gene's racing t-shirts were very special. In the Hanover Biathlon, Gene placed in the top ten. This was extraordinary because there were many professional racers there and he was very proud of his achievement. Gene shared that he loved the competition – it drove him to succeed.

The handkerchief in the lower corner of the quilt was from a Biathlon held at Lake Marburg in Hanover, Pennsylvania. It was a 3-mile run followed by a grueling 27-mike bike race and concluding with another 3-mile run. On the handkerchief, there is a reference to Gene's hero Lance Armstrong, three-time winner of the Tour de France.

In the upper corner, Gene selected a reminder of a very important race that was near and dear to his heart – the Shiloh 1-Miler. This was a benefit race held by his church with proceeds going to ALS research. The Halloween t-shirt was selected for Gracie because she always liked it and said Halloween was her favorite holiday. The t-shirt from the Museum of Scientific Discovery race was important because Gene crossed the finish line in 1st place.

He was active in sports and recreation and was able to coach soccer with the West Manchester REC league. Because his father had not been able to coach his teams when he was growing up, he was extremely proud to be part of this organization to share his love and passion for sports with both of his own children.

Gene was an avid Baltimore Orioles fan. Living in York, Pennsylvania, it was inevitable! When Gene would wear his Orioles "1954 American League" t-shirt, Gracie would crawl onto his lap and point at the third player in the front row and say, "That's you, Daddy." The shirt with a "G" insignia was added to her quilt and she always pointed to it and said, "That stands for Gene."

This quilt was made with love, and love is the emotion that exuded from Gene to everyone who knew him.

"The quilt Jenni made for me out of my father's t-shirts is one of my most precious belongings. To this day – over 15 years since my dad has been gone – I sleep with it every night. It is a warm reminder that his love is still with me. The stitching Jenni created of my father's face is perfect. My quilt is an amazing tribute to his memory that I will keep for the rest of my life." *~Gracie*

BALTIMORE
Baseball
CLUB
ORIOLES
Gabriel -
The Original!
Premier Running
1999
York
Miler
MICKEY
WEST
MANCHESTER
TOWNSHIP
RECREATION
LAKE MARBURG
BIATHLON
Red Hot
2001
Shiloh
One Miler

Gabe's quilt.

RON'S STORY

by Jennifer Vauk

Ron Vauk at Naval Academy.

Ron was the youngest of nine children, born and raised in Nampa, Idaho, to Hubert (Cubby) and Dorothy Vauk. He left Idaho after earning an appointment to the U.S. Naval Academy where he received a Bachelor's degree in political science in 1987. He served six years on active duty as a submarine officer and later on the staff of the Commander Submarine Force, Atlantic Fleet. His deployments included tours on two fast attack submarines, the *USS Glenard P. Lipscomb* and the *USS Oklahoma City*.

After retiring from active service he joined the Naval Reserve in 1993. Ron later joined the Applied Physics Laboratory (APL) in 1997 and earned a Master's degree in Technology Management from the University of Maryland in 1999. At APL he served as assistant supervisor of the Operational Assessments Group where he led projects to develop new and emerging technology and programs in support of the Navy's tactical and operational missions and led a series of training lectures to guide new staff toward a better understanding of the Navy. I met Ron while he was still in the Naval Academy.

We were married at the Academy in August 1987. It would be ten years before we were blessed with our first child Liam.

Ron was serving as the Active Watch Commander at the Pentagon Naval Command Center on September 11, 2001, the second day of his annual two-week active duty Navy Reserve training, when American Airlines Flight 77 crashed into the western façade, taking his life and the lives of 183 other patriots. Shortly after the tragedy, in November of 2001, our daughter Meaghan was born.

The memories of Ron are captured in all the fond thoughts from moments we enjoyed – memories we can only now internalize in our deepest thoughts and

Liam's baptism, with Jen, Ron, and godparents.

remembrances of him. But the sound of his voice, his sharp wit and humor, his infectious smile and spirit will forever be fresh and penetrating in our minds.

Meaghan and Liam with their grandmother, Ron's mom.

Because Liam was old enough to remember, he is now particularly emboldened by his father's spirit and patriotism. He expressed these sentiments to me recently when he remarked that the quilt was a reflection of his dad and the closeness they shared.

Meaghan has family stories, photos, visits to the 9/11 Pentagon Memorial and the 9/11 Memorial Museum in New York City and other echoes of his presence that surround and remind her of those precious times which she could not share. These memories and reflections are very tangible to her because they are warm thoughts she will carry with her through life – stories that will one day be told to her own children.

Ron was a devoted husband, a caring and attentive father, and a devout Catholic who was always ready to help family and friends. He made the most of every moment of every day. These are the traits and characteristics of a man that will be forever captured in our memory.

Meaghan, Jen, and Liam Vauk.

Ron's presence in our children is inescapable. And now, thanks to the skills and efforts of Jenni, his spirit and character are captured indelibly in the quilts painstakingly sewn together with pieces of his clothing. All those things that were ordinary and normal to his professional and leisure attire are now so special because they provide a connection to the man, husband, and father, and certainly a patriot lost but never forgotten. That was a cold time in our lives but the quilts now warm our bodies and comfort us with the memory of this wonderful man who will live forever in the hearts and souls of our children, family, friends, and shipmates.

We enjoy our freedom because of him. A life well lived will never be forgotten and these treasured quilts will always lie at the foot of their beds.

Meaghan and Liam with their quilts.

PEGGY'S STORY

by Lynne McDaniel

Lynne's mom and dad.

There's no better feeling in the world than knowing your mom is always there for you. I believe one of her life goals was to always be an integral part of her children's lives. Peggy Lou (Shaub) Shirey was born during the Great Depression on September 9, 1935. She was the twelfth of thirteen children. Mom often told stories of sharing a stuffed animal with her siblings and only receiving an orange at Christmas time.

She never knew her grandparents. She wanted to be an "old maid" schoolteacher until she married her high school sweetheart. Mom gave up her job as a secretary to stay home and raise her six children – five sons and one daughter. After nurturing us, she cared for her grandchildren on a daily basis while we pursued dreams and made a living.

A mother holds her children's hands for a while, but their hearts forever. The memories my mother made with me

Lynne and her brothers.

remain near and dear. Recollections of these wonderful times keep my heart happy.

Holidays and birthdays were always big celebrations. As children we may have received inexpensive or clearance items for gifts, but they were especially chosen for each one of us and given in love. Some of my early memories include dressing up like Indians and having a family pow-wow, camping, singing, playing games, watching Disney specials, reading, and participating in scouting events. Even with only one household income, my parents made our childhoods magical and memorable. These traditions have continued into adulthood and on to our grandchildren.

My mom was always reaching out to others to bring sunshine to them. She loved to send cards, write letters, and share pictures with those who needed a smile. Quotes were collected, stories written, and books read to be shared with her friends and family. Mom kept a diary for 56 of her 69 years and wrote blessing journals about things she was thankful for.

There are moments big and small when a mom makes all the difference in the world. Close to the end of her life she wondered aloud, "What have I done during my life that was important?" I was quick to answer, "Most importantly, you have been the best mom and grandma anyone could ever ask for. You have had a powerful impact on who your children and grandchildren are now and will become as they continue to grow."

"A life goal accomplished, a purpose completed is a living legacy to behold."

Family photo with mom and dad.

Love you, Mom. Thank you, Mom. Miss you, Mom.

I was given Jenni's name at a quilt show in York, Pennsylvania, when I inquired about finding someone to make a memory quilt. Each of the squares she crafted has a significance.

The angel in the center is because Mom not only collected angels, but she was a lovely person – an angel. She continues to bless my life daily as only an angel could. Mom collected and shared uplifting, positive quotes with many people. The squares with quotes on the quilt were meaningful to me because this is how I feel she touched and impacted my life. All other quilt squares are selected from her favorite clothing.

Even though my mom lives on in my heart and I feel her presence in my life, I wanted something to look at to remind me of her. I had a hard time getting rid of her clothing or anything she owned because I am very sentimental. The memory quilt helped me to move on in the grieving process and hold onto the positive impact she had on my life.

This quilt currently hangs on the wall across from the crib in the grandchildren's nursery in my home. Because I feel my mom was an angel on earth and now an angel in eternity, she can watch over her great grandchildren while they are in my home. Every time I look at the quilt, I smile. It warms my heart to know she is always with me and with those she would have loved as much as I do.

Lynne's quilt.

OUR TESTIMONIAL

by sisters Jayne Maas & Barbara Moore

A friend had quilts made by Jenni, so she gave us her contact information. My sister and I decided to make the trip to her studio in Pennsylvania to talk about making quilts for each of us from our parents' clothing and other items. One of the funniest times we were there was when her dog pooped in front of the door while we were talking.

There are simply no words to express "thank you" for the labor of love in making these healing quilts for my sister Barbara and me. We feel so much joy when we share them with others and when we run our fingers over each square remembering our mom and dad as they wore the clothing or used the items in their house. It is a celebration of their love.

Jenni and her work hold a very special place of honor in our family.

Barbara's quilt.

Jayne's quilt.

PARTING WORDS

If you have experienced the loss of a loved one, it may bring you healing to have a memory quilt or pillow made from their favorite clothing.

To learn how, visit Jenni's website:
www.theworkofmyheartquilts.com

Or contact the author by email at:
quiltinglady@hotmail.com

Made in the USA
Middletown, DE
07 October 2017